The Blueprint *for* A New Education

The Blueprint *for* A New Education

Empowering Self-Mastery and Selfless Service For The Common Good

TAISHA LALANAI RUCKER

ONE HUMANITY PRESS

ONE HUMANITY
PRESS

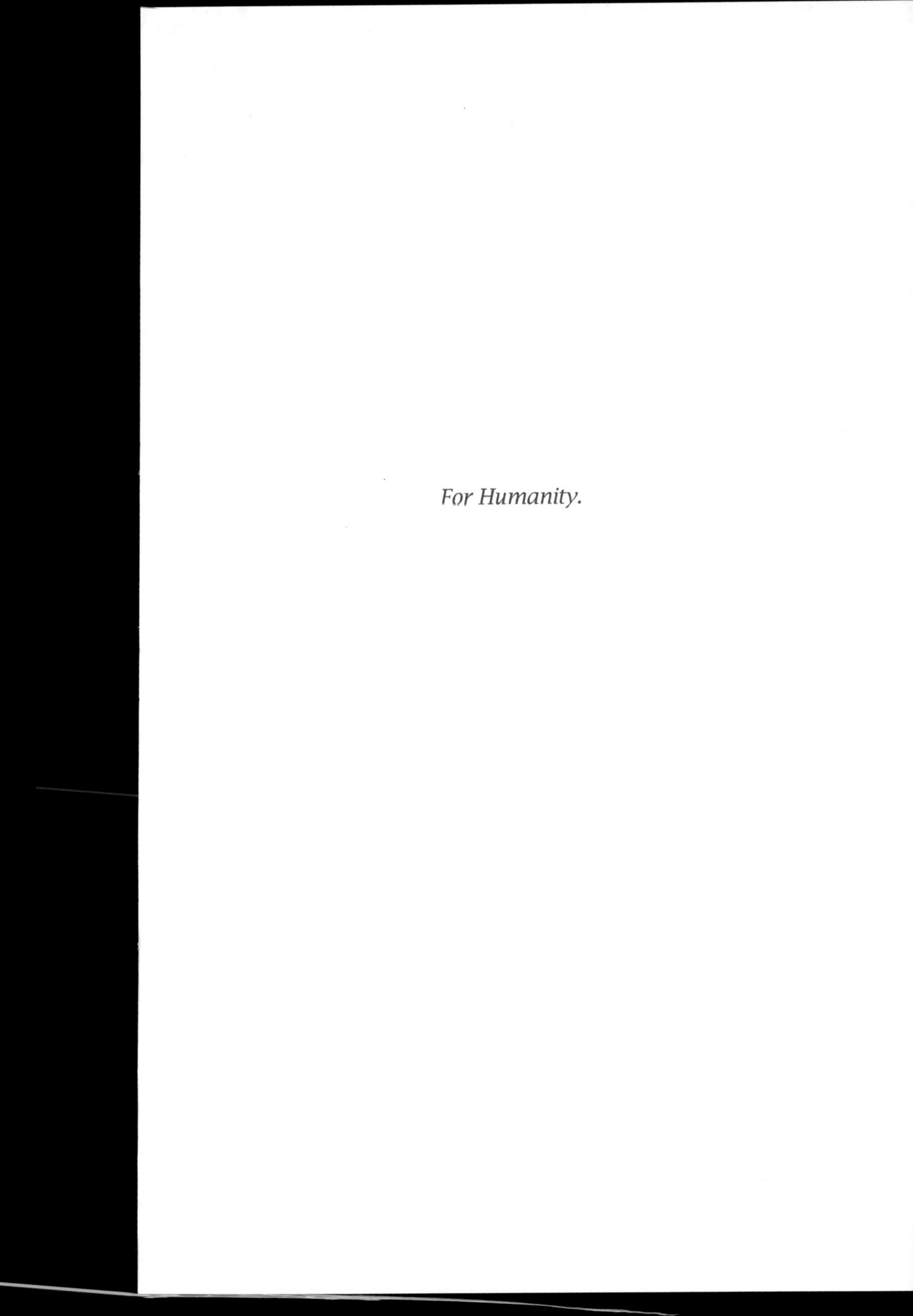

For Humanity.

TABLE OF CONTENTS

FOREWORD

IN TIMES OF profound uncertainty and relentless change, the search for guidance often leads us to those who stand as beacons of wisdom and clarity. Yet, today, amidst the throes of global upheaval and crises of conscience, the voices we once turned to for direction echo the uncertainty felt throughout society. Once seen as stalwarts of assurance, leaders now grapple openly with the complexities of our shared challenges, often mirroring the very confusion of those they seek to guide.

Amidst the turbulence of our times, the imperative for a new educational blueprint is unmistakable. Its foundation is not just about knowledge acquisition but also about self-mastery and selfless service for the common good. Taken to heart, it can help us navigate these uncertain times, transform our approach to cultivating citizens and leaders, and kindle a beacon of hope for our potential to become a more perfect expression of the Good, True, and Beautiful when united by a shared vision that serves the good of the Whole.

Within these pages, you will encounter a compelling argument for embracing a new educational paradigm that transcends the superficial trappings of authority and compliance. This is not just a theoretical vision, but a transformative force born of experience, understanding, and an unwavering love for humanity. The new education calls us to rise above the noise of the present, guiding us to seek out those whose wisdom springs from a profound commitment to serving the greatest good for the greatest number. It lays the groundwork to cultivate the next generation of self-aware, self-disciplined, creative, and enlightened citizens and future leaders, sparking a transformative journey that can reshape our nation and world for the better.

This blueprint challenges us to redefine our expectations, casting aside outdated paradigms and embracing an educational model that celebrates collaboration, compassion, and a deep-seated responsibility to the Whole.

As we navigate these destabilizing times, I cannot overstate the importance of redefining education's purpose. This book serves as both a manifesto and a guidebook, offering not just reflections but also practical steps on how we can nurture and begin to lay the foundation for a new education that equips the next generation of leaders and enlightened citizens with knowledge, spiritual clarity, and moral courage to use it wisely.

By embracing this blueprint, we acknowledge that we are both teachers and learners. Armed with this knowledge, we can establish a practice of daily living that becomes synonymous with humility, insight, and unwavering dedication to the common good. The power to bring about this change is not in some distant future, but it lies in our hands, here and now.

May this book inspire and empower all who dare to envision a brighter tomorrow through education that empowers, enlightens, and renews the spirit of humanity.

> *The idea of democracy, the ideas of liberty, equality, and fraternity, represent a society in which the distinction between the spiritual and the secular has ceased, and as in Greek theory, as in the Christian theory of the Kingdom of God, the church and the state, the divine and the human organization of society are one.*[1]

---

[1] Dewey, *The Early Works of John Dewey, Volume 1, 1882 - 1898,* 248.

1

THE BLUEPRINT

THE GOAL OF *The Blueprint for A New Education: Empowering Self-Mastery and Selfless Service for the Common Good* is to provide clarity on the fundamental issue in our current approach to education, demonstrate how a common good education can revitalize education's capacity to bring out the best in everyone and inspire you to create and experiment with those new ideas that will inevitably provide the basis for a new education better suited to the needs of today's humanity and our planet.

This blueprint sets forth a framework that:

- Defines a common good education.
- Identifies the root causes of education's current problems.

- Anticipates pushback to the transformation needed to reimagine education based on self-mastery and selfless service to the Whole.
- Simplifies an understanding of human development to equip educators, parents, and others to bring out the best in all children.
- Outlines a pathway to begin an effective transition to a common good education.

Let's begin by stating the question the blueprint strives to answer because if we ask any ten people what they believe the goal of education is, we will likely get at least ten different answers. Today's ideologies about education's objectives differ significantly. Some say that education should help students gain the necessary skills to get a job; others argue that not only are economic skills needed but the practical skills of daily life, which include balancing a checkbook, voting, paying bills, learning to drive, etc.; and still others— especially us humanities graduates—would argue that education's primary goal is now and has always been to enlarge students' capacity to make sense of the world so that they can be helpful to the world.

As with so many things, there is some truth in each of these pronouncements, exacerbating our inability to collectively arrive at a single educational goal that can serve humankind in every school, city, nation, and worldwide.

Yet that is the goal to which the blueprint aspires. So, the question I pose with the hope of being able to find a workable answer to ignite inquiry and collaborative solutions among educators, parents, and leaders is this:

> *How do we design or redesign education to develop each person's highest potential in response to world need and inspired by a shared vision for human and planetary betterment?*

As we continue our exploration, we should consider three aspects of this question. These include what is best for the individual, humanity as a whole, and our planet and the many lives within it.

Who Benefits?

1. Individuals.
2. Humanity as a whole.
3. Our planet.

Thus, we can begin to understand the basis of a common good education as one that develops the individual's capacities and awareness by rightly relating them to other human beings and the life of our planet.

Defining our current educational "Problem" essentially describes what is preventing education from adequately meeting the needs of the three entities that should benefit from any educational process: individuals, humanity, and the planet.

When education fails to consider the well-being of any of these three entities—individuals, humanity, and the planet—in its aims, it inevitably undermines the welfare of all.

INDIVIDUALS

The main goal of education should be to cultivate and enhance the potential of each person. When education systems overlook the physical or spiritual aspects of students' lives, individuals may struggle to reach their full potential or fail to consider their connection to others and interdependence within society. Failing to align inner aspirations with external accomplishments can increase stress levels, mental health issues, and a sense of futility, diminishing our quality of life, agency, and motivation for practical cooperation within families and society. Additionally, not bringing out the best in all children and instead elevating only a few and relegating many to unfulfilling lives creates a workforce that is less innovative, less engaged, and less capable of addressing complex challenges.

A lack of material resources can lead to elevated stress and related health issues. Moreover, a sense of disconnection can result in depression, anxiety, cognitive decline, as well as a reduced sense of purpose and motivation. Even among those who achieve outward success, there may still be a feeling of emptiness, resulting in a loss of meaning, stunted ethical and moral development, and a spiritual void inflaming their sense of isolation or separateness from society. This disconnection impacts individuals and weakens the social fabric, diminishing trust, civic participation, and goodwill, ultimately impeding collective progress.

HUMANITY AS A WHOLE

Education plays a crucial role in fostering a sense of community, social responsibility, and global citizenship. When educational systems fail to instill these values, it can lead to a fragmented and divided society.

The lack of emphasis on empathy, cooperation, and understanding among diverse groups can exacerbate social inequalities and tensions. An education system that neglects collective well-being can contribute to a world where mistrust and conflict are more prevalent, undermining the progress and stability of societies globally.

THE PLANET

When education ignores the importance of planetary stewardship, permitting unrestrained accumulation of resources by some individuals and nations at the expense of others, it leads to severe outcomes for both individuals and humanity.

Environmentally, it results in resource depletion, habitat destruction, and biodiversity loss, contributing to climate change and environmental degradation. These changes negatively impact individuals' health and livelihoods through increased pollution, food and water scarcity, and natural disasters.

Socially, unchecked resource accumulation exacerbates inequalities, creating a wider gap between the wealthy and the impoverished, leading to social unrest and conflicts over dwindling resources.

Economically, it can destabilize markets and lead to economic crises as finite resources become scarce.

Considering the planet's welfare is crucial, as failure to do so could lead to unsustainable living conditions, jeopardizing global stability and the ability of future generations to thrive.

By ensuring that educational aims promote the well-being of individuals, humanity, and the planet, we lay the groundwork for a more sustainable, equitable, and prosperous future for all. Overlooking any of these dimensions undermines the overall health and progress of society, underscoring the need for an integrated educational strategy that values and fosters the interconnected welfare of all entities.

2

THE PROBLEM

THE MAIN CHALLENGE in modern education is essentially between adhering to a predominantly materialistic worldview emphasizing external factors rather than embracing one that includes our more subjective, spiritual nature. We are not merely flesh and bones but thinking, feeling, imagining, aspiring, and, ultimately, spiritual beings striving for betterment.

- A largely materially focused education prioritizes accumulated facts, testing, job and career ambitions, college majors that will pay the most money, etc. It, therefore, focuses our achievements and aspirations towards conformity to present ideals, whether these are the most advantageous to human and planetary well-being. Further, by ignoring or denying the dual aspects—material and spiritual—of ourselves and the world, we fail to fully comprehend our nature and lack the requisite knowledge and commitment needed to integrate and make ourselves and the world whole.

- In contrast, a spiritually guided education not only equips us to navigate the present but also empowers us to envision and create a more fulfilling future. It encourages us to harmonize our spiritual and material aspects, or what some refer to as our personality and Soul, or lower and higher Self, leading to a more balanced and enriched life.

- Enlarging our focus to include the replenishing and limitless subjective aspect of our nature (i.e., the immanent God or Spirit within us) unlocks new capacities alongside a growing identification with the Common Good.

- A spirit-centered education recognizes what is and what can be and takes deliberate steps to cultivate human beings capable of fully participating in creating a new and better world from the inside out.

A common good education supposes that the field of education can and must add its quota alongside religion and philosophy to further human development not solely focused upon our outer, objective lives but also our inner, subjective being.

3

THE SOLUTION

THE BASIS OF a new education is a common good education, which develops each person's highest potential by expanding their awareness and mastery of themselves and their environment as they learn to see themselves as an integral part of a larger whole to which they increasingly desire to give their best.

This redefined concept of education holds the transformative power to shift our focus from the material to the spiritual, from the finite to the boundless. It encourages us to explore the immaterial aspect of our being, thereby reimagining the very goal of education.

Expanding our self-knowledge is the key to unlocking our

interconnectedness with all, be it the people of different nations or the nonhuman kingdoms that help shape our planet. This deepened understanding not only connects us to all that exists but also inspires us to serve.

As a result, service will not need to be something cultivated externally. It will not be a burdensome duty but a spontaneous impulse that arises from within, driving our actions and our desire to better ourselves. The basis for education can, therefore, motivate us to serve selflessly and continuously develop the best within us to expand our capacity to serve others.

4

SELF-MASTERY

THE RESULT OF a common good education for the individual is self-mastery, encompassing three stages of integration and fusion of the individual within the Whole. These are:

1. *"Know Thyself."*

   Consistent with the Delphic Oracle, "Know Thyself," individuals are taught to understand their desires, feelings, and thoughts as the impetus for their actions.

2. *"Know the Self,"* linking each to Humanity.

   Next, individuals are taught to recognize their subjective spiritual Self, which relates each to Humanity as a whole.

3. *"Know the One,"* linking us to all nations and the whole of our planet.

Lastly, individuals are taught to see themselves as part of the one planetary Life, which provides the necessary incentive to formulate the right thoughts and take the right actions that improve the lives of others and the world of which they are an integral part.

Questions for Reflection and Group Dialogue

1. If my students understood education as the primary way to know and develop themselves as part of a greater whole, how would this change how they think about school?

2. Think about a time when you stopped trying to get a student to achieve a specific outcome and focused instead on helping the student understand what about themselves stood in the way of them achieving their goals. Consider the results of this attempt (failure is an option!).

3. What is one thing you might do differently in your classroom or school to cultivate students' desire for self-mastery to equip themselves to serve others?

4. When considering the students who often fall through the cracks or are underserved because of disability, race, gender, and so on, how might a common good education enable schools to serve them better and themselves to find an improved sense of belonging? Mastery? Purpose?

5. Can you think of examples in your interactions with youth that indicate their desire to expand their knowledge of themselves and the world to be part of the solution to our problems? Describe one or more of these examples.

5

REFLECTIONS

CONTEMPLATING AND DISCUSSING the reflections on the concept of a common good education allows us to realize that while it may seem like a drastic shift from our current educational focus, the essence of this idea is subtly present just beneath the surface. It's essential to recognize that beneath the façade of students' antisocial behaviors, growing anxiety, instances of bullying, disengagement, and various other challenges lies a deep yearning for more than just academic knowledge. What students genuinely seek is a method to master themselves and the world they live in, to live purposefully, and to find fulfillment that transcends mere material survival.

Is it possible that much of the turmoil we currently observe in education—student mental health issues, student-to-teacher aggression, teacher disenchantment and burn-out, book bans, a push for prayer in schools, and increased patriotism, curtailment of race-based initiatives including affirmative action and diversity, equity, and inclusion programs based on a perception—right or wrong—that such programs further divide us—all stem from a shared desire to create an educational system that engenders a sense of higher values upon which a new and more unified culture and civilization can take shape?

The Blueprint attests that the demand for a new education is already observable within the cracks of modern education, letting in the light that can illuminate new possibilities.

Emphasizing the development of the whole person, integrating students' inner and outer lives fosters a learning environment where students feel valued, understood, and connected. They learn to navigate the complexities of life with confidence and compassion, cultivating a sense of responsibility towards themselves and others.

Moreover, a common good education recognizes the interconnectedness of all aspects of human experience. It encourages collaboration, critical thinking, and practical goodwill to all, preparing students to tackle the pressing challenges of our time. Through this integrated approach, education becomes a powerful tool for personal and collective transformation, enabling individuals to thrive in a rapidly changing world while contributing to the greater good.

In essence, the shift towards a common good education is not just a response to the current educational shortcomings but a reimagining of what education can and should be. It is about creating a system that nurtures the potential of every student, helping them find their place and purpose in the world and equipping them with the tools to lead meaningful, fulfilling, and purposeful lives.

To navigate this tumultuous period, we must undertake a twofold task addressing immediate reactions and long-term strategies for societal betterment. Firstly, it is essential to calm the reflexive and prescriptive "solutions" that various individuals and groups propose as definitive answers to our collective desire for improvement. These quick fixes often stem from a narrow perspective, exacerbating division rather than fostering unity. Instead, we should encourage a more reflective approach, promoting dialogue and understanding among diverse viewpoints. Secondly, we must present a framework for this new education as a unifying foundation to serve the good of the whole and each part.

Implementing a common good education must benefit the greatest and the least of us. In doing so, we spark a new and confident vision for the future that reassures people with various needs and demands of its potential benefits and builds a sustainable path forward, fostering a sense of shared purpose and mutual trust.

6

THE SIX PILLARS OF THE NEW EDUCATION

WE CAN AGREE that part of the difficulty in transforming education is the fact that some things work more or less for most students, making it easier to blame students, teachers, parents, community violence, racism, and other facets of life on education's inability to adequately prepare ALL students for a healthy, happy, and purposeful life. As a result, calls to "revolutionize" or "radically transform" education often fall on deaf ears because there is sufficient benefit to a consistent few to give the appearance at least of its foundational integrity.

Further complicating things is that we can't agree on the purpose of education. If we were to ask ten people to define the purpose of education, we'd likely get at least ten different answers. Each perspective would emphasize some one thing: to teach people to think for themselves, to prepare them to get a good paying job or to do work that matters, to help them learn to work well with others, to love God and country, to bring out the best in them.

There is contentious positioning over what we should value most—national pride, high-paying jobs, social mobility, diversity and inclusion.

Trying to appeal to one or another of these interests creates a fragmented educational system like what we see today. This provides an opportunity to identify a simpler approach that can serve everyone's needs.

Focusing on self-mastery ensures every child reaches their full potential by becoming self-aware, self-directed, and self-expressing.

Focusing on selfless service for the common good ensures every child recognizes that they are part of something bigger through relationships with others and the environment. They learn that they are not alone but can depend on others and be depended upon to improve conditions for themselves, others, and perhaps the world as a whole.

The table below identifies crucial differences between traditional education's focus and the six pillars that comprise the new common good education in which every child, irrespective of ability, can learn to take the next step available on the road to self-mastery and selfless service to the whole.

THE SIX PILLARS	
Traditional Education vs **Common Good Education**	
Overemphasis on Grades: Focusing on grades and academic achievement can overshadow the importance of creativity, critical thinking, and emotional intelligence.	**Real-World Application**: Promotes understanding of the world and more deeply integrates knowledge, providing opportunities for students to gain and demonstrate skills that have a real impact.
One-Size-Fits-All Approach: Traditional education often fails to accommodate student interests and individual needs, leading to disengagement.	**Interest-Based Learning**: The advantage of interest-based learning is that it leverages students' innate desire to help them achieve, creating a virtuous cycle of self-determination.
Top-Down Control: Hierarchical decision-making by policymakers and administrators, positioning teachers as primary sources of knowledge where students are expected to passively receive information rather than actively engage in the learning process.	**Autonomy and Responsibility**: Balancing student autonomy and responsibility fosters critical thinking, self-discipline, problem-solving, and time management skills, which help them take ownership of their actions and decisions while promoting personal growth and maturity.
Teachers as Technicians: High stakes testing and scripted lessons with predetermined outcomes make teachers complicit in eroding students' creativity, critical thinking, and intrinsic social consciousness, which makes them aware of and desirous of responding to the needs of others, their families, and their community.	**Teachers as Emancipators**: Nurturing a universality that unites all people, nations, and life, teachers cultivate students' understanding of the actual and the ideal and their individual and collective capacity to become integral co-creators improving life for themselves, their families, communities, and world, inspiring personal growth, recognized interdependence, and collective well-being.

Six Pillars cont.	
Disciplinary Measures: Traditional school disciplinary methods can be punitive and authoritarian, focusing on compliance and control rather than teaching self-regulation and responsibility.	**Self-Regulation and Self-Mastery:** Prioritizing self-mastery equips students to regulate their emotions, persevere despite obstacles, and delay gratification to achieve their goals, helping them learn the skills foundational to long-term success, happiness, and overall mental and physical well-being.
Darwinian Social Dynamics: School social dynamics often create artificial student hierarchies based on popularity, cliques, peer pressure, stereotyping, and competition. These peer groupings can lead to adverse outcomes such as bullying, ostracization, and loneliness. Dominant students may exert control over others, while marginalized students struggle to fit in, resulting in power imbalances and social exclusion. A lack of inclusive culture further exacerbates these issues, impacting students' mental health and overall well-being.	**Prosocial Relationships:** An education that promotes the common good creates an environment where students recognize that some peers may have a greater aptitude for responsibility and service while others may need extra guidance, positive role models, and further development. By valuing each student's unique journey and potential, we can encourage mutual respect, compassion, and collaboration, cultivating a supportive and harmonious learning community of continuous give and take.

7

CASE STUDY: LEE*

Name changed to protect privacy and maintain confidentiality.

Overview

Lee, a sixteen-year-old young man, was previously dismissed from an all-boys residential program for unknown reasons. He later returned. Our program implemented trauma-informed care (TIC), including residential, educational, and clinical components. For those familiar with the Adverse Childhood Experiences (ACEs) scores, our student population's average was four.

Lee demonstrated anxiety, low self-worth, and defensive avoidance, yet he naturally attracted peers due to his quiet, pleasant, and witty demeanor. Despite initial compliance, Lee's behavior deteriorated, and he faced potential dismissal. This case study explores how the six pillars of a common good education—real-world application, interest-based learning, autonomy and responsibility, teachers as emancipators, self-regulation and self-mastery, and prosocial relationships—can be effectively leveraged to help students like Lee become self-aware, self-directed, and self-expressive in ways that benefit themselves and the common good.

Real-World Application

Lee struggled with traditional schooling's passive learning approach, which often leads to disengagement, especially for students who prefer experiential learning. Unfortunately, the program's hands-on, practical learning experiences, including campus jobs, agriculture, raising sheep, and woodshop, failed to appeal. I assessed that he had existed in a persistent state of disillusionment about schooling and education for quite some time, which would naturally require an equal and persistent corrective to begin to make a positive impact in a demonstrable way. Most of our other students were not so disillusioned and greatly benefited from the creative ways our staff scrambled to help students apply concepts in real-world contexts. By emphasizing real-world application, students can see the relevance of their education, increasing their engagement and motivation.

Interest-Based Learning

I recognized Lee's potential and suggested he take the California High School Proficiency Examination (CHSPE). This approach was interest-based, acknowledging his proficiency in areas like Math and his aversion to the traditional school environment. The idea was to provide him with an alternative path to obtain a high school diploma, which he had promised his mom he would get. Although Lee didn't take the CHSPE, the opportunity to do so proved to be a revealing experience that validated his seeking to create a unique opportunity for him to reach his goals and made him face up to the fact that the primary obstacle to his success was not his parents, school, teachers but himself. After presenting a clear path forward to him, Lee realized that he would need to discipline himself and improve his work ethic to take advantage of the opportunity, which he was not at that time prepared to do. Yet, knowing what he needed to become to move ahead was a powerful lesson that would serve him beyond high school.

Autonomy and Responsibility

When pitching the CHSPE idea, Lee showed a twinkle of recognition, suggesting a resonance with his inner Self. Helping students awaken to their true selves requires patience and a desire to integrate our lower and higher nature. A recognition between souls bypasses the usual personality distortions that can distract us from the immediacy of recognition of our shared brotherhood, evoking respect, reverence, and knowledge of how we might help them. Such a soul recognition fosters immediate trust in the guide from the one seeking help in recognition of equality from that within them that knows itself to be a coequal part of a greater Whole. When the students and teacher meet as souls, irrespective of the subject taught or proffered lessons, there will be a formidable exchange of knowledge on many levels that may take the student a lifetime to absorb and work out into their experience fully. Once contact soul-to-soul was made, a definite change was apparent, even if not permanent.

After obtaining his mother's approval, Lee took initial steps toward self-mastery, actively seeking me out for guidance, demonstrating his burgeoning sense of autonomy and responsibility. This process of self-discovery and growth takes time, and it's important to remember that the first contact with this higher Self is just the beginning of a journey that requires patience and persistence to stabilize to the point that it can be relied upon and trusted without fail.

I facilitated similar transformative encounters for other students, guiding them to connect with their higher Selves—that part of us that is inherently wise, liberated, and resilient. This connection empowered them to handle life's obstacles with newfound confidence and clarity. The resulting shift was unmistakable, immediately redirecting their lives towards a more positive and purposeful path. These experiences demonstrated the profound impact of aligning with one's higher Self, evidencing a deep and lasting change in attitudes, behaviors, and overall life direction.

However, it would be unwise to expect immediate and drastic changes from every child, just as it would be unrealistic to demand that every adult change their behaviors, habits, or ways of thinking simply because they now have a better understanding. Genuine and lasting transformation takes time. By being patient and not seeking instant results, we can and will equip young people with a new competence and interpretative faculty that will serve them long past their association with us, helping them navigate and improve their conditions and the world around them for the long term. This enduring impact demonstrates the effectiveness of our approach.

Teachers as Emancipators

My approach to Lee was always playful yet no-nonsense. We had more than a few "come to Jesus" conversations as we tried to help him navigate the new demands of becoming autonomous and responsible for managing his time and studies in preparation for the CHSPE. Observing him in other classes and engaging with him through playful interventions like blocking his online access to non-educational content helped build a rapport. By advocating for exceptions like allowing him to wear his hoodie due to a skin rash, I demonstrated understanding and empathy, positioning myself as an emancipator rather than a disciplinarian. This approach helped create a safe and supportive environment for Lee to explore his potential and gauge his readiness to embrace and chart his own course.

My goal became to help him discover the Self within, that when recognized and integrated with the persona, would empower him to choose for himself, act on his own volition in ways that would benefit him, and, in due time, be an asset to his family, to our school, and perhaps even in the world at large.

Self-Regulation and Self-Mastery

Lee's journey towards self-regulation and self-mastery involved making him aware of his inner Self and its capacity to inspire and direct his actions. As a liberating guide for students and having progressed beyond the stage awaiting their receptivity, I already knew the higher Self to be inherently wise, omniscient, and a most capable ally in navigating life. By fostering Lee's connection and integration with his higher Self, I knew that he could begin to alleviate his anxiety, develop self-worth, and become a self-directed and responsible individual. Although he did not achieve the specific milestone of passing the CHSPE, the process initiated the opportunity for a more profound, lasting change.

In human development terms, I aimed to help Lee become an integrated personality, meaning that he could see himself more clearly, recognize his capabilities, and awaken a desire to channel those in some direction that would benefit him. In effect, he would begin to take the steps that eventually lead each of us to become an enlightened personality dedicated to serving the common good.

Prosocial Relationships

Over several months, Lee and I developed a strong relationship based on mutual respect and understanding. This relationship was crucial in helping him feel supported and valued. Using humor and direct communication, I connected with Lee personally, which helped him feel seen and heard. This prosocial relationship was essential in establishing trust, which allowed me to help guide him toward self-awareness and self-expression that benefits himself and the community.

Conclusion

Lee's story illustrates how the principles of common good education can be applied within our current system to foster the development of both high-achieving and underserved learners. By emphasizing real-world application, interest-based learning, autonomy and responsibility, teachers as emancipators, self-regulation and self-mastery, and prosocial relationships, educators and other caring adults can help students become self-aware, self-directed, and self-expressive in ways that serve them, their families, communities, nation, and world.

8

EDUCATE TO LIBERATE

L IKE MANY YOUNG men, Lee struggled under the traditional pillars of education with its overemphasis on passive rather than experiential learning stemming from a cultural adherence to the preeminence of authority, dogma, and accepted doctrine as the approved basis for the transference and acquisition of knowledge. Indeed, these have their place during those earlier stages through which humanity as a whole has passed before education was widespread and many millions began to think for themselves and become increasingly capable of making sense of the world absent the need to rely on rulers, the intelligentsia, religious leaders, and other select few.

Today, however, a new educational framework must take into account the strides humanity has made and account for most people's desire, even if not their realized capacity, to think for themselves, develop discernment, and test the integrity of knowledge—past and present—presented to them through experiment and experience.

A new education, therefore, recognizes a shared divinity among all people due to being part of the one planetary life, albeit at various levels of adequately expressing their divine nature or what some call the Self or Soul. This subjective and still, for many people, young and old, largely undeveloped aspect and capacity is the key to awakening our full potential. Identification with the spiritual Self expands and deepens our understanding of the world and ourselves, unlocking each person's ability to *know thyself, know the Self,* and *know the One.*

The process of integration and fusion is the key to individual and collective development. It leads to goodwill toward others and a desire to serve our world by developing the best within us.

By nurturing recognition of this inner *Self,* aware of its group relations inclusive of the whole of humanity, alongside the persona or personality most often emphasized with its likes and dislikes, strengths and weaknesses, and peculiarities, we can help every child awaken not only to their capability but also to their responsibility.

Each individual is in service to the group—groups in service to humanity—humanity in service to the living planet. Developed in this way, we will create a humanity whose members willingly and selflessly choose to contribute their best to the whole according to human and planetary needs. Artificial divisions along national, racial, gender, and socio-economic lines will steadily dissolve as the contributions made by the One Humanity throughout all fields of human enterprise begin to mitigate the harm we have unitedly caused.

Many educators are already using some combination of these six pillars— real-world application, interest-based learning, autonomy and responsibility, teachers as emancipators, self-regulation and self-mastery, and prosocial relationships—but may not know how you're doing it or how to apply it in every case and for every child consistently.

The Blueprint aims to inaugurate a basis for a new education, preserving the best of our modern education while establishing the six pillars of a common good education as the building blocks to create transformative outcomes for all students wherever they are in their development and expression as human and divine beings.

A common good education prioritizes young people's self-awareness, self-determination, and self-expression, equipping each, according to their level of responsiveness and ability, to choose of their own volition the definite outcomes they seek and the steps to take to achieve their goals for the good of the Whole.

Shifting education's focus to emphasize its liberatory quality can accelerate our ability to create better student outcomes. A common good education approach can reduce classroom management challenges for overworked teachers by engaging students in meaningful, self-directed learning. For concerned parents, it ensures that their children are not just academically proficient but also develop into conscientious, compassionate, and intelligent citizens. By integrating these qualities, we foster students better equipped to navigate life's challenges, demonstrate goodwill, and promote right human relations. Ultimately, this education cultivates a generation committed to stewarding planetary resources purposefully to further liberate humanity, creating a brighter future for all.

Striving to integrate our inner and outer lives, combining the subtle and the mundane, which have been falsely separated into material and spiritual aspects in our consciousness, is the key to overcoming individual and collective fragmentation. Often, what currently exists closes our eyes to what could be.

In a world where what we do frequently takes precedence over who we are, it is crucial to recognize the dynamic livingness of the Spirit behind appearances. By doing so, we encounter the group conscious Soul, which seeks to guide and direct the self-centered personality, thereby clarifying our perception and willingness to participate in realizing the shared vision for peace and plenty, which is humanity's destiny.

Equally, provocations arising from within—a new idea, a feeling of wanting and deserving more, a new choice—or external—a closed door, a failed relationship, a shattering of confidence in one's ability, a crisis— are part of the totality of human experience and when handled rightly can lead us to better conditions and lives.

Too much focus on external factors and past traumas overlooks the potential for personal growth within each of us. While it is essential to acknowledge and address external circumstances and historical wounds, our efforts should not stop there. True empowerment involves equipping individuals, especially children, to tap into their inner wisdom, helping them take positive steps beyond the scope even of our ability to assist.

By nurturing self-awareness, self-direction, and self-expression, we can help individuals realize their potential and transcend the limitations imposed by their environments and past experiences. This approach encourages proactive engagement with life, where each person becomes an active participant in their journey toward personal fulfillment and eventually collective success.

Therefore, the basis of the new education should aim to strike a balance between offering necessary external support while simultaneously guiding individuals to tap into their intrinsic resources. By doing so, we enable them to take positive steps forward, ultimately leading to sustainable personal and societal growth that extends beyond the reach of even the most generous external assistance freely given.

We must learn to save by awakening the savior within each child. It is the true source of vision for the individual, nations, and humanity as a whole. It is the soul in each of us that unites, organizes, and intelligently directs all people and nations to take those steps and actions that are essential to our collective well-being.

Without vision, the people perish.

Educators can do their part to help restore humanity's capacity to envision the good of the Whole and develop the best within us in service to the common good. This is the proper task of education: not simply to imbue facts of what has been but to ignite the vision for what can be.

By teaching, we don't just educate; we liberate!

9

LIGHTING THE WAY

PRIORITIZING SELF-MASTERY means we educate children to be *self-aware*, helping them develop the best in themselves, *self-directed*, helping them choose a vocation or career, and *self-expressing*, helping them live responsibly among their families, peers, communities, nations, and the world.

Embracing a common good education means redefining the goal. The goal of education, then, isn't to learn Math or English, get perfect attendance, get a good job, or learn resilience or how to do hard things even if you don't like them.

Instead, we must strive to build a system of education that recognizes that results that equip people to be effective, cooperative members of our society come naturally to a person beginning to" Know the Self," identifying themselves as an integral part of a greater whole.

When education prioritizes integration and fusion, we awaken inner capabilities alongside the capacity to envision the part each can play in serving the whole. The fruition of this realization is necessarily more limited for some than others. Still, it is nevertheless a foundation upon which each of us can build a life of purposeful living.

Then, recognizing inner capacities alongside a vision for serving others motivates us to learn Math or Science, stick with difficult things until we succeed, recognize obstacles as opportunities to bring out our best, and know how best to overcome them.

There are countless examples throughout history of people with limited resources, capabilities, or socially validated intelligence who have nevertheless recognized what they could give to the world because they identified with human needs and strained themselves to give their best to serve.

These individuals, driven by compassion and a profound understanding of others' struggles, transcended their limitations to contribute meaningfully to society. Their dedication and determination not only uplifted those around them but also inspired generations to believe in the transformative power of compassion and perseverance, proving that the impact of one's actions can far outweigh the circumstances from which they arise.

There is something inherent in witnessing others' pain and suffering and a reflexive desire to help that brings out our best. A new education presumes this about each person, whether they are currently capable or desirous of expressing this intrinsic relatedness.

People of all grades and levels exist in our society in terms of consciousness. So-called bad actors are simply less cognizant of their relationship to the whole, often acting from narrow self-interest or ignorance of broader consequences.

However, through education, increased self-knowledge, and a growing understanding of interconnectedness, individuals can evolve their consciousness, becoming more aware of their impact on others and the world around them. This awareness fosters a collective responsibility to nurture a society where goodwill towards others guides our actions, promoting harmony and well-being for all.

When instead we insist that children obey or we manipulate them to obtain an immediate change in behaviors even if it doesn't stick, we inadvertently undermine children's ability to know and trust themselves, stifling their progress and delaying the realization of the outcomes we seek.

Rather than learning through experience, including the inevitable missteps, we insist on capitulation to our demands to "ack right" while undermining the process by which human beings learn to discern right from wrong based on experience and the consequences, good and bad, that naturally arise because of our choices.

To create a nation and world of enlightened citizens, we must raise individuals aware of their human and divine nature and understand how to become whole through serving the whole. Thus, education can cultivate an informed citizenry to select leaders whose wisdom, understanding, and incentive to collaborate demonstrate their capacity to govern. In turn, an enlightened public will freely choose to be governed by these leaders because, by discovering their own selves, they recognize each person's place within the Kingdom of God or Hierarchy of Souls, which includes identifying those farther ahead on the path and therefore capable of assisting them on their journey as well as those behind for whom they can provide help.

The beauty of prioritizing integration and fusion is its simplicity. It recognizes each of us as a point of light within the fabric of the universe. Some points shine as brightly as the stars lighting the night sky, while others may be dimmer, yet each has its unique place and potential to blaze forth.

By embracing integration and fusion, we acknowledge the interconnectedness of all life and the inherent worth of every individual. This perspective fosters a sense of unity and shared purpose, where every point of light contributes to the greater whole. It encourages us to support and uplift one another, understanding that our collective radiance depends on the growth and empowerment of each community member.

In this harmonious blend, we find unity in diversity. We exist within a tapestry where every thread, regardless of its present brightness, can shine more brilliantly. This approach promotes an environment of inclusivity and mutual respect, where the potential for personal and communal growth is boundless. It's a reminder that in such an environment, each of us can grow and contribute, fostering a sense of belonging and collective responsibility.

Ultimately, prioritizing integration and fusion reminds us that our true power lies in our ability to come together, become a brighter light, and engage with others to ensure their growing luminosity. In doing so, we pave the way for a future where everyone can realize their potential, transforming our shared universe into a beacon of hope, love, and infinite possibility.

Before we can proceed, we must prepare ourselves to face opposition. The resistance won't likely stem from a lack of desire for education to foster self-aware, self-directed, and self-expressive individuals. Instead, it may arise from the fact that transforming education involves replacing the established, limited outcomes of our current material-focused system with the broader, though unproven, potential of one that includes subjective or spiritually oriented approaches.

It's crucial to remember that most resistance will come from uncertainty and fear rather than a flat-out rejection of new possibilities.

10

ANTICIPATING AND OVERCOMING PUSHBACK

CHANGE IS HARD. There are many reasons that people fear change. Of course, some pushback stems from a desire to hinder human progress. That's a fact. But most people, even those who desire change, will often experience grave discomfort because of legitimate questions and concerns.

Resistance to transforming modern education to incorporate teacher roles as liberators and enhance student autonomy can stem from various factors, including uncertainty, fear of the new, institutional inertia, resource constraints, and accountability pressures prioritizing quantifiable outcomes. Cultural norms and traditional views on education, concerns about losing classroom control, and a lack of understanding of new methods also play significant roles. Additionally, teacher preparedness, parental concerns about college and career readiness, political and social resistance, and general risk aversion further contribute to the reluctance to embrace these educational changes.

When introducing change, people often have legitimate concerns that may appear as resistance but are rooted in genuine questions and anxieties. These questions can include:

- How will this change impact my role and responsibilities?

- How will we introduce a new educational goal of this magnitude alongside current expectations from educators, parents, and students?

- How will success be measured when education relies heavily on grades, test scores, and other quantitative criteria?

- How does this change align with our organizational values and mission?

Addressing these questions transparently and empathetically can help alleviate concerns and reduce perceived resistance to change. Looking at some specific examples may also help clarify anticipated resistance, probable causes, and responses.

Teacher Pushback: *I just want to teach Math!*

Some teachers will insist that it's their job to teach the subject, and that's it. We could ask if they prefer to teach Math to a student who hates Math because they don't believe that they can learn it or to teach someone who lacks the skill but understands its necessity and is willing to dedicate themselves to learning it.

By focusing only on getting students to do this or that, we reinforce their sense of self-doubt and fragmentation, resulting in the rise of mental health issues we see among teens today and low self-esteem. They learn to act without understanding how they think or feel. Therefore, they fail to equip themselves to bring their whole being to any activity, missing out on recognizing and revealing their inherent capabilities.

Foundational subjects such as Math, Science, English, and History play a crucial role in making knowledge of the world accessible to students. However, their disinterest is not in seeking to understand the world but often in memorizing and reciting facts disconnected from their interests and present experience of the changing world in which they must take up their place.

The new education paradigm assumes that students are inherently interested in understanding the world around them. When their interests are nurtured, they will naturally seek answers that involve the usual academic subjects. Consequently, cultivating each child's desire to know themselves is the starting point for a desire to understand their place in the world, learn how to relate to others, and eventually become a practical agent of goodwill.

Parent Pushback: *My kid needs a 1570 SAT score to get into Stanford! Let me worry about their inner lives. You are there to make them learn Math, English, History, Spanish, Physics, etc.*

Our commitment to student learning and knowledge acquisition remains unwavering. However, we are now placing a greater emphasis on the process of personal integration. This shift in focus acknowledges that by nurturing integrated and soul-infused personalities, we awaken students to their inner potential and better equip them to chart their life paths and achieve their goals.

Integral to a common good education is awakening each child's desire to understand that they are thinking, feeling, and doing human beings who, when integrated, mastered, focused, and directed toward the good of the whole, make possible higher achievement for the individual and society.

Traditional Social-Emotional Learning (SEL) practices are valiant but prescriptive attempts to make students "good." The basis of a new education focuses on personal integration in an environment and through relationships that demonstrate the *GOOD*.

In other words, we can no longer rely on the mantra "Do as I say, not as I do." Our ability to be *good* and exhibit the right relations with our colleagues, students, families, and others determines precisely how much we can cultivate the *good* in our students.

Eventually, our concept of right relations will expand to incorporate all people and the planet. There isn't a set curriculum that can accomplish the goals of integration and fusion. Right relationships, cultivated and demonstrated, bring out the good in us and others.

Embedding the idea of BECOMING WHOLE TO SERVE THE WHOLE in

our classrooms, schools, and throughout our relationships can spark a renewed educational approach that will help each person reach their highest potential and make our world better because of it.

"Liberté, égalité, fraternité" (French for "liberty, equality, fraternity") underpins our democratic traditions, shaping how we see ourselves and each other. These principles highlight the importance of freedom, equality, and brotherhood in creating a just society. They also remind us that true democracy involves more than just political structures; it requires a commitment to fostering these values in every aspect of our lives. Education, as a cornerstone of democracy, must reflect and promote these ideals to cultivate citizens who can sustain and advance a fair and harmonious society.

As an emancipator, the teacher cannot, in good conscience, serve solely as a subject matter expert or skills-based trainer beholden to business needs. While these qualities are useful, they do not encompass an educator's full responsibility.

A teacher's primary duty is to nurture critical thinking, creativity, and a sense of justice in their students. They must inspire learners to question the status quo, seek truth, and develop a deep understanding of their values and beliefs. By doing so, teachers empower students to become active, informed citizens who can contribute meaningfully to society.

Furthermore, the teacher cannot be an authoritarian extension of states, economies, religions, or parents. To do so would undermine the principles of liberty, equality, and fraternity. Education must be a space for students to explore diverse perspectives and develop informed opinions. Teachers should encourage dialogue, respect for differing viewpoints, and the pursuit of knowledge of what has been and what is presently possible to nurture the common good. This approach respects each student's individuality and fosters a sense of community and shared purpose, which is essential for the health of any democracy.

In this light, the role of the teacher extends beyond imparting knowledge and skills. It involves cultivating a universal consciousness that recognizes the inherent dignity and worth of every individual. By nurturing a collaborative learning environment, teachers guide students towards self-mastery and selfless service for the common good. They help students understand their interconnectedness with all people and the planet, inspiring both personal growth and collective well-being. Through this transformative approach, education becomes a powerful force for social change, grounded in the democratic ideals of liberty, equality, and fraternity.

Ultimately, the teacher's position as an emancipator aligns with the highest aspirations of democracy. It calls for an educational system that prepares individuals not just for economic productivity but for meaningful participation in a just and equitable society. By embracing this role, teachers can help build a world where liberty, equality, and fraternity are ideals and lived realities for all.

Educators have always been partners within society rather than today's presumed antagonistic foes, serving as mentors, guides, and the conscience of young people searching for identity and belonging. They are an important link between the family and community, between a narrow self-interest and a universal compassion, and between the personal and political, playing a crucial role in shaping the future.

The liberating teacher meets every child where they are and creates those opportunities and conditions that release them into new fields of experience, developed capacity, and purposeful living.

Parents, teachers, mentors, and business leaders must share a commitment to the next generation to ensure that each child has all that they need to develop the best within them, equipping them to give their best to the world in service to the common good. It takes a village because, ultimately, we are each an individual personality and an expression of the universal One Soul. We are *unity in diversity*. We are both the Whole and the part.

Of course, any caring adult can assume the role of a liberator by ensuring the focus of their interactions with others, including youth, derive from a desire to educate through teaching, guiding, mentoring, and relating in ways that confirm the principles of liberty, equality, and fraternity, striving to bring out the best in others based on their own pursuit to recognize, interpret, and express the divine evolutionary Plan for which the greatest good for the greatest number is the aim.

The true goal of education is to cater to the diverse needs for knowledge across all aspects of human life. Education, therefore, is the responsibility of all selfless, wise, and understanding individuals attuned to the needs of all people to grow in wisdom and committed to their own enlightenment. This calling includes parents, teachers, mentors, spiritual leaders, business figures, and anyone else who demonstrates their capacity to act as a trustworthy guide to humanity through the totality of their living.

Administrator Pushback: *Teach whatever you want to teach so long as students' test scores keep going up!*

In its truest form, education is meant to liberate, open minds to new possibilities, foster wise perception and response to world circumstances, and nurture creativity and personal growth. However, the current educational landscape has become increasingly mired in a fixation on tangible and measurable outcomes. This bureaucracy's narrow focus on standardized test scores, grades, and quantifiable achievements often overshadows education's broader and more profound purposes.

This outcome-driven approach tends to promote a one-size-fits-all model of education, ignoring individual students' diverse needs and potentials. Proper education should recognize and cultivate each student's unique talents and passions, empowering them to pursue their own paths and contribute meaningfully to society.

Even administrators who buy into the need for change will find it especially difficult as sponsors of the present educational systems to facilitate the needed changes. However, they, along with a group of committed educators, play an integral role in moving the needle and facilitating the necessary growth and progress.

In working with my principal, who was admittedly averse to change, I learned to approach him with my revolutionary ideas, and a viable step-by-step plan of implementation that he could see with clarity could help provide some practical solutions now *and* offer the long-term potential benefits I knew were possible.

Forward movement must be a collaborative process constantly adapted while keeping the end goal of human progress in mind. Education must stop subjugating itself to the more strictly material concerns that reinforce estrangement from oneself and others through attentiveness primarily to what one does rather than to who one is, focusing as it does on competition over cooperation and standardization at the expense of creativity.

Instead, education must reclaim its inherent liberating capacity. It is through education that we can free the human spirit. Through education, the dim light of knowledge becomes the searchlight of wisdom that sees and embraces ever-greater truths. Through education, a human being eventually arrives at the right self-knowledge, self-determination, and self-expression.

Many youths I have worked with often do not demonstrate the drive to acquire, possess, and conquer whatever stands in the way of selfish accumulations. In fact, they are frequently lost because the new ideal of education has yet to reach them, and the old materialism doesn't appeal to them.

Others expend their energies trying to fit into a decaying materialistic world of competition and scarcity but are exhausted, anxious, and unable to fill a growing void where the soul in us should live.

Therefore, a new education is needed: an education that helps usher youth and young adults closer to the goal articulated under the Delphic injunction: "Know thyself."

In fact, the world as it currently exists is primarily the work of individuals working as personalities, unconscious of themselves as souls, even while acting on its inspired ideas. All of humanity's groundbreaking and innovative ideas can be traced back to the selfless part of our nature whose vision is only in service to the highest good for the greatest number.

Creating a new world demands that we educate people as souls, not just as separate individuals, to work in cooperation with others. In this way, the vision of the whole that guides the soul in each of us can work through our diverse personalities, serving according to the soul's vision (which is untarnished by individualistic and selfish desires). Then, people will meet within the world in alignment with the work that is theirs to do in service to the greater good.

This can begin in earnest within education by creating those methods and processes that simultaneously develop *self-conscious* and *group conscious* human beings who have increasing awareness and mastery of themselves and their environment, are aware of themselves as members of the whole of humanity, and are capable, therefore, of envisioning and implementing the new ideals that can create a new and better world based on a shared understanding of the greatest good for the greatest number. In doing so, we can restore education's role as a powerful catalyst for personal and societal transformation.

When such an education is implemented, it will provide three things for the child thus educated:

It will provide children, beginning in early life, with a sense of *direction* that eventually indicates vocation and avocation, aiding the choice of a career.

It will *draw out* the best in children, making each a center of "life more abundantly" wherever they find themselves. It will enable each child to attract to themselves those who can help them and those whom they can help, or those who are responsible for aiding them and those whom they must eventually responsibly serve.

It will make children positively *creative*, enabling them to link within themselves the renewing spirit of life, group consciousness, and the results of their own efforts in service to the One Humanity of which they increasingly know themselves to be a vital part.

Student Pushback

Working with a high-needs population provided a unique opportunity to experiment with a common good education's six pillars: real-world application, interest-based learning, autonomy and responsibility, teachers as emancipators, self-regulation and self-mastery, and prosocial relationships.

Traditional education was inadequate in engaging and educating a significant portion of our student population, revealing its inherent limitations and inefficacies. This widespread ineffectiveness demanded that we innovate.

Observing the lackluster outcomes of conventional approaches, many of today's educators find themselves in similar situations, increasingly hesitant to rely on more traditional methods and needing an approach upon which to build.

Educators, students, and many parents are clamoring for a more streamlined and impactful approach, despite appearances and evident resistance, that can serve as a springboard for change, unifying them around a shared and motivating goal that better addresses learners' diverse needs and facilitates personally meaningful and socially purposeful learning.

Considering this, we can expect measurably more vigorous pushback from high-achieving students. *Why?* By some accounts, the highest-achieving students—those who get into top colleges and universities and take high-paying positions on Wall Street, Big Law, or Tech—are

#Winning. They have the most to "lose," or so it seems.

The same burned-out, anxious, and depressed students looking for another way will likely vociferously reject a common good education. They will say:

1. What does self-mastery have to do with me getting a job? Graduating?

2. Please tell me what I need to know or do to finish school or get into college.

3. I have to get good grades, or my parents will... or I won't be able to get a good job... or I'll never get into grad school... or as one student interviewed for the film, "*Try Harder!*" tracking one high schools' college admissions journey says, "And I need to go to one of the top 20 colleges because otherwise, I'm not going to be doing anything significant."

The thread running through the anticipated pushback is due to our clinging to life's objective, materialistic side. We pretend that results matter more than the ideas, intent, and attitudes that cause them.

Societal norms and educational systems prioritizing external measures of success over internal fulfillment and purposeful living lead many people to experience a variety of responses, including imposter syndrome. For those whose outward success is inconsistent with their sense of self, this creates a looming self-doubt even in the face of realized success.

Others, like me, may confront a pervasive sense of self-estrangement at some point. This disconnect often stems from societal conditioning that prioritizes the pursuit of fame, wealth, power, and influence as markers of success.

From an early age, our educational systems emphasize these external metrics, guiding us toward careers and pathways that promise expedient acquisition and material consumption. Consequently, the professions we choose or the work we're forced to do often diverge from the deeper yearnings of our authentic selves, those urges seeking expression in ways that contribute meaningfully to the greater whole.

Our livelihoods, dictated by economic imperatives and societal expectations, frequently lead us astray from the life seeking to manifest through us. This divergence creates a profound inner division. We find ourselves torn between the demands of external validation and the quieter yet insistent voice within that seeks genuine self-expression and contribution. This inner conflict is further compounded by an educational model that increasingly diminishes introspection and personal insight, instead emphasizing conformity to external standards and benchmarks.

As a result, we become susceptible to the cacophony of outward influences—societal norms, media messages, and peer and family expectations—which often drown out the whispers of our inner wisdom.

The outer world, with its relentless emphasis on material success and comparative worth, becomes the primary measure of our value. In this pursuit, the rich terrain of our inner world is silenced and overshadowed, leading to a disconnection from our true selves.

This self-estrangement has profound implications for personal well-being and social, economic, and political harmony. Despite outward success, individuals may experience a sense of emptiness, feeling unfulfilled and disconnected from a more profound understanding of purpose.

Moreover, at a societal level, this disconnection fosters a culture of competition, comparison, and superficiality, eroding compassion, goodwill, and collective well-being.

Addressing the pervasiveness of this self-estrangement requires reexamining our values and educational priorities. It calls for a shift towards nurturing a new education that honors both external achievements and internal growth—one that encourages individuals to cultivate self-awareness, self-direction, and creative expression fueled by a sense of purpose aligned with their unique strengths and self-initiated desire to serve the common good.

By reconnecting with the world within, individuals can reclaim agency over their lives and contribute authentically to their communities and the world.

Overcoming self-estrangement involves recognizing and honoring the voice within that speaks of deeper aspirations beyond mere acquisition and consumption. It entails creating educational and societal environments that foster introspection, authenticity, and a sense of interconnectedness. Only then can we begin to bridge the gap between the external measures of success and the profound fulfillment that comes from living a life aligned with our truest selves.

In doing so, we will nurture human beings who know that security is not dependent on outer success but develops in progressive stages as we learn to bridge the gap between who we are and who we hope to be.

This practice involves aligning our current self with our ideal Self, finding harmony within ourselves and the planet where "we live and move and have our being."

Without this conscious awareness, people remain vulnerable to doubt, uncertainty, and a profound sense of futility. Lacking agency, such individuals can never be all they can be and, as a result, cannot be held accountable for refusing or neglecting to take up their share of responsibility as family and community members and national and world citizens.

A process of integration and fusion is the key to helping individuals move farther along the continuum to mastery. First, individuals become integrated personalities driven by personal ambitions and aims and express themselves dominantly in one or another field of human endeavor. At this stage, an individual is mentally focused, replacing the previous dominance of the feeling nature that controls many.

Over time, as the personality persists in its efforts to grow and increase its influence, it will learn valuable lessons that lead to identifying as an essential part of a larger whole. These experiences will bring it closer to the higher Self as it works towards realizing the planetary evolutionary Plan and its goal to unify all life on our planet to reveal perfect Truth, Beauty, and Goodness.

The soul must eventually displace the personality as the director and organizer of life because it is our true group conscious identity. It is capable of initiating activities through each enlightened personality for their benefit and the benefit of the whole.

These expansions of consciousness and empowered self-expression take place over long periods but, when begun in earnest, can transform individuals, communities, and nations.

The key to overcoming doubt lies in understanding and reconciling our present selves with a perceived ideal Self, aware of Its interdependence with and committed to the good of the Whole. This means recognizing and embracing the full spectrum of our identity—acknowledging both our human and divine aspects.

When we achieve this inner harmony, we cultivate a sense of wholeness and confidence unshaken by external circumstances. Thus, our inner security becomes a profound and stable foundation independent of outward success, empowering us to face life's challenges with resilience and grace.

It's important to acknowledge that a common good education doesn't guarantee the tangible outcomes students, parents, and teachers have grown accustomed to expecting from education, primarily personal, material success!

For those of us who believe that this new approach can help free education from an outworn framework, however effective it has, in some respects, proved to be, we must go forward with compassion, understanding that those who stand to be most helped are necessarily those who are likely to be the least receptive initially.

Taking the time to address the concerns of all stakeholders requires clear communication, evidence of success, and a phased, supportive implementation approach.

The Right Relations Protocol, outlined later, can help us have the necessary conversations and discover and collaborate with others with whom we share a "unity of purpose" to build a new and improved education that serves the humanity we are and are becoming.

11

THE COMMON GOOD ROADMAP

NOW THAT WE'VE defined a common good education, briefly reviewed its application and outcomes in the life of a typical high school student, and covered some of the usual pushback we're likely to get from teachers, parents, students, and administrators, it's now time to outline the progressive developmental stages and milestones foundational to the integration and fusion process.

One approach involves slow evolutionary development, which consists of trial and error. We make mistakes, damage relationships, and pay the price for the harm we've caused, but eventually and gradually, we adapt. Having achieved all we desire and still finding ourselves unhappy, we seek out another way: the way of the common good.

An alternative approach, foundational to the new education, is centered on accelerated, conscious growth. It takes into account the needs of the larger community from the beginning. The goal is to minimize our negative impact and learn from our mistakes as we grow to become more capable and eager to contribute positively to our families, schools, communities, nations, and humanity.

There are essentially two pathways for human development. The first is through *Trial & Error*. It is the slow but eventually successful process by which we learn and grow as human beings. We selfishly go about our lives trying to fulfill our desires, often at others' expense.

At some point, we realize that having all we desire still leaves much to be desired. We then focus less on ourselves, allowing us to align with others, and we turn our attention toward achieving a group good, sacrificing what we desire for our families, groups of which we are a part, and so on.

Many of us are familiar with the path of *Trial and Error*, wherein we make mistakes, damage relationships, and pay the price for the harm we cause.

But there is another way.

The second pathway of *Accelerated, Conscious Growth* is one in which we still seek to fulfill our desires. Yet, we do so because, increasingly, what we want is what is most needed by those with whom we've aligned ourselves, eventually enveloping the whole.

Through a conscious evolution, we learn to recognize that personal development ideally can equip us for ever greater service. We realize that we can grow slowly but surely (and, often painfully) in isolation or strengthen and accelerate development for all of humanity by recognizing our interconnectedness and fitting ourselves to serve in an ever-widening capacity.

If we accept that conscious and, therefore, accelerated growth is a worthy endeavor, one way to explain and chart progress is through the Common Good Roadmap.

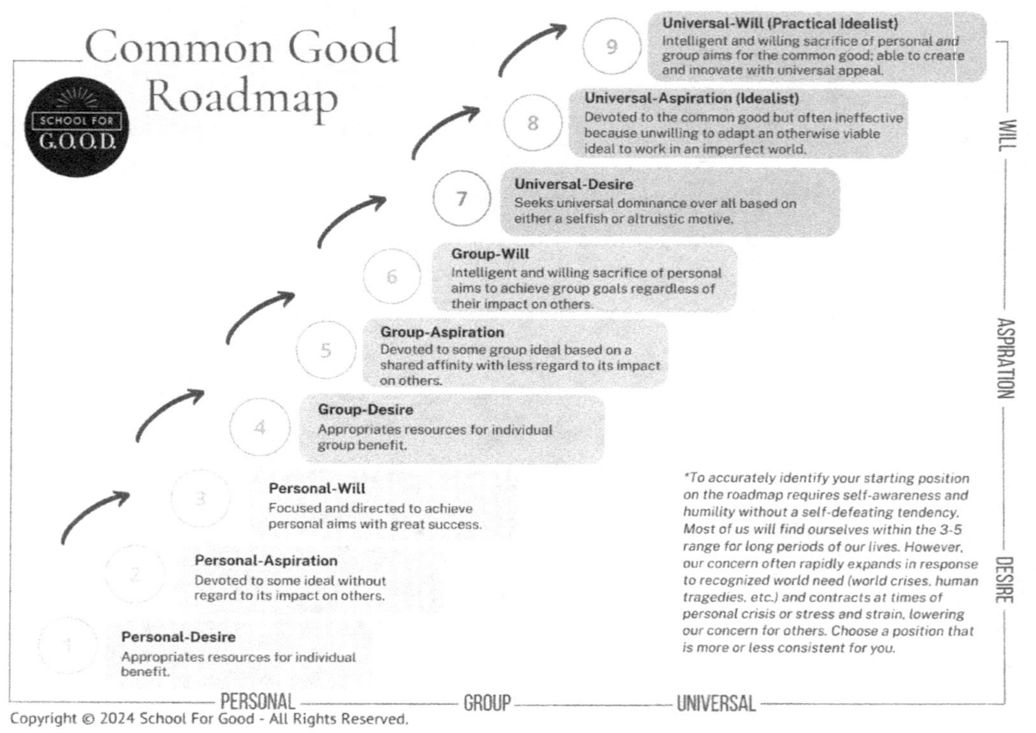

*Visuals are available for download at www.schoolforgood.org/handouts.

This roadmap can guide us in understanding our place and the place of others within the broader context of an evolving awareness and responsiveness to the needs of the whole. As we develop as conscious, *will*-ing individuals, we progress from selfishly registering and asserting our needs to include those of the people we love and with whom we share affinities. Ultimately, in this lifetime or another, we evolve to selflessly prioritize the needs of the whole.

Through conscious development, we can eventually locate ourselves between stages 3 (Personal Will) and 5 (Group Aspiration). To put this in context, I will describe the optimal stage—the Universal-Will stage—and its lower reflections, the Group-Will and Personal-Will stages, leaving you to work out the other levels independently.

At the top of this pyramid is the stage of **Universal Will**, which humanity strives to express correctly. We can understand it as perfect Love, comprising an intelligent and universal *will-to-Good*.

At this stage of development, an individual may not hold a position of power, but they are sought out by many for their wise counsel on personal and professional matters. Their influence is extensive, yet their contributions may not always be formally recognized or acknowledged. For the organizations and groups lucky enough to have them as part of their team, they serve as the conscience or the soul, quietly influencing, guiding, and patiently waiting behind the scenes for others to recognize the vision and insights that become increasingly available to all striving to love and serve humanity. They aim to bring forth new ideals to overcome existing obstacles and inspire renewal for all.

At our current stage of development, humanity is becoming increasingly capable of reaching the midway point, known as the stage of **Group Will**. This stage allows us to express a coordinated, intelligent, and understanding form of *Good*-will towards everyone.

Many people expressing this stage of consciousness are willing to sacrifice themselves to achieve a group ideal, whether for good or for ill. When encountering such individuals and groups, we can remind ourselves that the impetus for their actions tends toward selflessness although, as yet, limited to a group goal specific to their group and its objectives rather than the good of the whole. This understanding can give us the needed perspective to see past our personal preferences and help others do the same.

The lesser stage, plainly observable in every nation and throughout every sphere of human living—social, religious, political, and economic—is inhabited by people at or near achieving the stage designated as **Personal Will**.

Individuals at this stage of development are often influential and well-known, leading some of the most powerful and successful companies, churches, and organizations today. They are highly effective at achieving their goals. Some may prioritize their personal ambitions over the well-being of others, while others struggle internally with the harm their actions may cause. These individuals often justify their harmful actions using language and strategies that make them seem acceptable to others. In doing so, they may delude and manipulate others to achieve their goals, like their more openly ruthless counterparts, but with a veneer of justification and acceptability. These individuals cannot respond to appeals based on a selfless will to serve the greater good because ambition and self-interest rather than a conscious connection to their higher Self drives them.

Of course, there is, thankfully, much variety of expression within each stage, and it is increasingly so among people who are integrated personalities.

Many self-conscious personalities are actively committed to doing good in the world but recognize that we are consciously wrestling with the choice between sacrificing our strident individualism in service to the common good and sticking with our personal and perhaps good-*ish* agendas.

Some are quicker to respond to humanity's cumulative and significant needs than others. Still, essentially, our examples of leadership tend toward the selfish rather than the sacrificing, as evidenced by a quick Google search, which indicates Darth Vader (Star Wars) and Gordon Gekko (Wall Street) in a list answering the question: *"Who are good leaders in movies?"*

By promoting the development of integrated personalities and emphasizing that individuals are part of a larger whole, common good education aims to reduce the excessive individualism that often creates divisions between people and their environment and others. Instead, the goal is to nurture individuals who can harness their fullest potential, becoming as organized and efficient as top business, religious, and governmental leaders, but with an unwavering dedication to the entire community's well-being because of their genuine love for humanity. This approach ultimately leads to a more collaborative and compassionate society.

Therefore, our aim in a common good education is to cultivate for everyone, wherever they find themselves on the roadmap, a sense of the destination that considers the good of the whole.

The goal isn't to eliminate any step but to make an accelerated forward movement possible to get us unstuck from our present circumstances, which display entrenched individualism and, as a result, widespread human and planetary suffering.

Maturing humanity can begin to move knowingly through the human developmental stages. Collectively, we aren't there yet, but we are evolving to be capable of thinking and acting according to a more integrated group consciousness, passing or having passed through the stage of beneficent self-consciousness, making us capably sensitive to and increasingly aware of the interconnectedness of life within our environment and universe.

As humanity matures, we can begin to develop each person more seamlessly and with intentionality through the corresponding stages of the Common Good Roadmap, collectively defined as PRIMARY (stages 1-3), SECONDARY (stages 4-6), and HIGHER (stages 7-9) Education.

Of course, few individuals will display a progression through all stages in a lifetime. However, humanity as a whole is evolving towards a greater capacity for goodwill and a desire for right human relations. This collective evolution is marked by an increasing ability to think and act with intelligence, understanding, and a commitment to the common good.

We now stand at the dawn of a new era, offering unprecedented opportunities for collective betterment. This new possibility hinges on our willingness to sacrifice personal desires, aspirations, and self-assertion to manifest a plan that benefits the whole. This shift towards a selfless commitment to the greater good signifies our readiness to embrace and actualize these higher stages of development.

To ensure collective advancement, we must work within the groups we serve to ensure they become aware of and align their goals with the common good. This alignment is crucial in addressing the pressing issues of our time, such as political divisiveness and discord, climate catastrophes, wars, social breakdown, and economic inequality.

When groups prioritize the common good, fostering dialogue and collaboration over conflict and competition, we can mitigate political acrimony and disunity. By focusing on shared values and goals, we can bridge ideological gaps and work together towards solutions that benefit everyone.

Climate catastrophes demand a unified response that transcends individual and national interests. When groups align their goals with the common good, they are more likely to implement sustainable practices and policies that address the root causes of environmental degradation, promoting long-term ecological balance.

Wars and conflicts often stem from a failure to recognize our interconnectedness and mutual dependence. By instilling an awareness of the common good within groups, we can encourage diplomatic and peaceful approaches to resolving disputes, emphasizing cooperation and mutual respect over aggression and domination.

Social breakdown is often a result of systemic injustices and the erosion of community bonds. Groups that align with the common good work to build inclusive, supportive communities that uplift all members, fostering social cohesion and resilience against division.

Further, economic inequality is a critical challenge that undermines social stability and prosperity. When groups prioritize the common good, they advocate for fair and equitable economic policies that provide opportunities for all, reducing disparities and promoting a more just and balanced society.

By ensuring that the groups we serve are aware of and aligned with the goals of the common good, we create a ripple effect that extends beyond individual actions. This collective alignment empowers us to tackle the complex and interconnected issues of our time, paving the way for a more harmonious, sustainable, and just world.

Mass Consciousness to Group Consciousness

Education, when viewed from the standpoint of humanity as a whole, is a transformative process. It liberates us from the control of mass instinct and self-serving intellect, ushering us towards an intuitive group consciousness.

Education illuminates the collective mind, facilitating an eventual enlightened Commons through which the will of the people will no longer reinforce selfishness and separateness but goodwill, sharing, and cooperation between and among all people and nations.

An enlightened Commons engenders people's willingness to see beyond their immediate interests and consider the welfare of others. This shift in perspective leads to a stronger sense of community and interconnectedness, where the focus is on mutual support and collective progress.

The will of the people, thus enlightened, begins to reflect these higher values.

There is a distinct difference between the "group mind" and the "mass mind." It is the difference between soul response and personal reactivity, between pure reason and personal feeling, between willing the *Good* and the divisive aims that keep us locked in numerous conflicts—capital and labor, college and non-college educated, black and white, urban-rural, democratic and communist.

"Mass mind" is the hive mind that encircles and engulfs us as long as we respond to life and circumstances primarily based on personal feelings. It mainly stems from the sensitive feeling nature that still controls many people and exposes us to waves of uncontrolled energy and misdirected mass feeling to which we are learning how not to react. The mass mind is, in fact, mass *feeling*, accounting equally for mob rule, unrestrained hilarity (distinguished from finding humor in the foibles of life experience), religious revivals, financial panics, and world wars.

These situations demonstrate how the mass mind (feeling) can lead to actions not guided by reason or higher principles but collective emotional impulses. Interestingly, individuals governed by their personal feelings can either be prone to succumbing to or taking a stand against the mass *feeling*. Opposing unchecked and misdirected energy nonetheless stimulates an equal and similar emotional intensity and response, perpetuating a cycle of reactivity and discord. In both cases, the feeling rather than the thinking nature controls.

The needed response to the impulsivity and irrationality of the "mass mind" is not opposition driven by an equally emotional reactivity but striving to transcend personal feelings through integration and fusion with the Soul.

From the plane of mind, *I* rule. This is the Soul's beckoning call to a humanity ravaged by personal, social, environmental, and global turmoil driven by selfishness. Upon the mental plane, the true individuality, the higher Self or Soul, controls. The personality is its creation, and after its due development, purification, and maturation, it becomes the Soul's agent, carrying out its goals for the good of the whole.

Thus, "group mind" refers to those individuals whose strong mental focus increasingly connects them to and allows them to be controlled and guided by the Soul, whose inclusiveness is absolute.

As more individuals integrate and fuse with their Souls, the collective consciousness begins to shift. The mass mind, characterized by impetuousness and irrationality, is gradually transformed into a group mind marked by goodwill, cooperation, and understanding.

Nations, too, are influenced by this process of enlightenment. As cohorts of citizens become sensitive to their higher selves through recognition and correct response to the shared vision for world betterment, they become a "group mind." This national and global group of world servers can be the necessary counterbalance to bring enlightenment to the masses everywhere.

Like individuals, nations become cooperative enterprises as countries learn to work together to address common challenges such as climate change, poverty, and conflict. They become driven by a shared recognition of our interconnected destiny and the understanding that the well-being of one nation is intrinsically linked to the well-being of others.

Education is a cooperative venture teaching the art of living through relationships that either help us become all we can be or distract or hinder our progression. Whether in the home, school, public square, churches, or workplaces, we teach others and learn how to be. Our primary lessons should help each person recognize their individuality and universality, relating each to all. Then, we will create a humanity dedicated to the welfare of all and increasingly capable of contributing to the uplift and well-being of all people everywhere.

How we interact with others, regardless of our role—as a teacher, parent, friend, mentor, manager, spiritual guide, government representative—must be understood and undertaken to demonstrate what is possible through self-initiated conscious development in our living and *be*-ness. Such development not only helps us discover our most authentic spiritual Self but also frees humanity from perpetuating cycles of win-lose, progress-regress, peace-war. All this comes from each person's efforts to identify with and serve the common good.

We are both teachers and students learning to live cooperatively on our planet and within this universe. Sharing and sustainability of planetary resources and their equitable use to advance the human race's freedom, equality, and fraternity through cycles of the appearance, dissolution, and reappearance of new and improved cultures, nations, and civilizations is our collective burden and purpose.

Our dual role as teacher and learner allows us to evolve continuously, learning from others and imparting our knowledge in a reciprocal cycle of growth. We are fortunate to recognize when we have encountered other souls farther ahead on the journey of self-mastery. Through their wisdom and experience, these individuals can guide us in further developing ourselves.

Even if they are not leaders in the traditional sense, they exemplify leadership through their presence, peace, and keen insight into human nature and world events. Their selflessness in sharing these insights, even when met with our resistance, plants seeds of truth within us. Over time, these kernels of wisdom germinate, allowing the "real" in us to recognize and resonate with the "real" in them.

In this way, we grow in community with others, forming a diverse support and learning network. Some in this community are ahead of us on the journey, offering guidance and inspiration. Others are striving behind us, looking to us for the wisdom and loving understanding we are also seeking to gain. Our shared experiences and insights create a dynamic and supportive environment where everyone can flourish. Schools, churches, community centers, workplaces, and other places and spaces can become centers of mutual healing, deliverance, and reciprocity.

By embracing our roles as teachers and students, we contribute to a collective journey of self-mastery. Whether we are giving or receiving guidance, each interaction deepens our understanding and fosters a sense of far-reaching affinity. This mutual growth enriches our lives, bringing us closer to our highest potential and creating a ripple effect that benefits the One Humanity and One Planet.

The adjacent graphic summarizes the three stages of human development that the new education should instill during primary school, high school, and higher education.

USING THE COMMON GOOD ROADMAP

for personal and group development

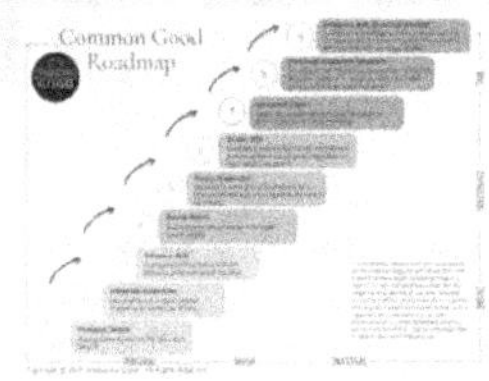

INTEGRATION & FUSION PROCESS

info@schoolforgood.org

The Common Good Roadmap helps individuals and humanity more closely manifest a higher divine perfection by recognizing where we are and the next step possible, leading from self-consciousness (personality integration) to group consciousness (soul-personality fusion) and eventually to universal consciousness.

PRIMARY SCHOOL

INSTINCT

Developing group sensitivity to internal and environmental impacts, preparing individuals to eventually live rightly within the world that IS and capable of visioning it as it should be.

HIGH SCHOOL

INTELLECT

Developing group capacity for self-directed, coordinated action to positively impact our environment, achieving *CGE-Stage 3* or **personality integration**.

HIGHER EDUCATION

INTUITION

Developing wise group application of knowledge based on an evolving understanding of future possibilities and present potential to establish the common good, achieving *CGE-Stage 6* or **soul-personality fusion**.

How might we present the Common Good Roadmap to individuals and groups to encourage its use in helping them realize their higher capacities through identification with the whole?

Three Stages of Human Development

- Primary education (ages 5 - 12) - INSTINCT

- Secondary education (ages 13- 18) - INTELLECT

- Higher education (ages 19+) - INTUITION

Let's contextualize the analogy of primary, secondary, and higher education applied to humanity as a whole.

These three divisions—primary, secondary, and higher education—roughly indicate the three stages of human development, leading from self-consciousness to group consciousness and eventual universal consciousness. In other words, these three stages cultivate human instinct, intellect, and intuition.

The time individuals enter and emerge from the primary, secondary, and higher education stages symbolically varies widely and over long periods because we each develop differently. Therefore, understanding each individual's accrued stage of development is needed to better guide them to accurate self-knowledge and onward to their next step.

Primary Education

The primary education stage should focus on developing the child's **instinct**, conditioning young people to be sensitive to their inner lives as well as the outer world, and creating what we typically refer to as a good moral foundation based on having a good temperament, treating others as they wish to be treated, and helping to make visible their true inner nature.

In short, primary school should cultivate children's imagination, making their vision for a better future possible and laying the foundation for the gradual transfer of acquired knowledge developed throughout the ages, transforming humanity into what it is today.

The realizable goal is a humanity that has developed a sensitivity to internal and environmental impacts, preparing them to eventually live rightly within the world that *IS* and capable of envisioning it as it should be.

Secondary Education

At the secondary education stage, which is the stage humanity—when viewed as a whole—has reached, children learn to develop, focus, and direct the intellect based on the previously developed sensitivity to the inner and outer worlds acquired as a result of development in primary school.

Instinct and intellect lay the foundation for proper personality integration so that a person becomes aware of how the world impacts them and their impact upon the world. They can then learn to become a coordinated individual capable of directing their thoughts and actions to bring about the good in their families, environment, and the larger world.

In short, high school builds upon prior learning to inspire integration within the individual of their physical, emotional, and mental aspects. Through experiment and experience, it teaches them the benefit of identification with others they contact and humankind, fostering a sense of belonging and connection.

The realizable goal is a humanity that engages in self-directed, coordinated action to positively impact the environment, thus demonstrating **personality integration**.

Higher Education

Higher education is the stage that will develop the **intuition**, which is the higher sensitivity to which the personal feeling nature eventually yields. This intuitive mechanism communicates and facilitates the higher Self's goals, which infallibly serve the good of the whole in the same way the intellect serves the lower self's aims and ambitions.

Intuition bridges between the personality and the higher Self, allowing individuals to access inner wisdom and clarity that align with universal truths and values. This intuitive awareness helps individuals perceive the interrelation of all things and make decisions that benefit the greater good rather than just the individual self.

When one is becoming an integrated personality (at the secondary education stage), intuitive moments begin to register that assist the individual in understanding those ideas that, throughout human history, have led stage-by-stage to a better world. As we learn to think, we are brought into contact with the evolutionary Plan unfolding upon our planet as it fuses all life expressions—planetary kingdoms and nations—into a unified, perfected Whole.

In short, higher education should cultivate intuitive recognition of emerging ideas leading to world betterment and the wise recognition and application of those ideas based on what is presently possible at any given time in human history in service to the common good.

The realizable goal for a maturing humanity is the wise application of knowledge based on understanding future possibilities and present potential, thus completing the **integration-fusion process,** linking past, present, and future.

Stage-by-stage humanity has and continues to evolve. A common good education provides a framework that allows us to grow consciously, accelerating the path to unity and manifesting a better world for all, fostering a sense of connection and shared purpose.

We can expect a common good education to make us aware of our subjective, spiritual nature and develop a humanity of *self-aware, self-determined*, and *self-expressing* individuals, groups, and nations who think and act increasingly to benefit the Whole.

12

RIGHT RELATIONS PROTOCOL

LASTLY, I WANT to share a tool that can be helpful in conversations and further the integration-fusion process for individuals and groups.

As I mentioned previously, using the Right Relations Protocol can help us collaborate with others based on recognizing a shared goal, benefitting the common good, and leading to coordinated activity while leaving individuals and groups free to grasp and implement those aspects of the evolutionary Plan they can register, interpret, and work out as they see fit.

Cultivating our shared ability to become sensitive and receptive to the vision unfolding for our collective betterment, seeking to work it out through cooperation with others similarly focused on intelligent, loving service to humankind, and refusing to prioritize the needs of the few above those of the many will help us create a better world that serves the *Good*.

There are always selfishly individualistic entities attempting to thwart humanity's progress and realization of unity. These malefic forces exist in every nation, class, race, and religion. They seek to reinforce our sense of separation and foment antagonism between people and nations. Transforming them requires a similar approach that I used when dealing with students' antisocial behaviors: an adapted Right Relations Protocol (RRP) (as outlined in *Unleashing the Good: How We Learn to Prioritize the Common Good Over Personal Gain*), which includes the following three steps:

Recognize the many paths to truth, resulting in *right understanding*. Recognize that each person, group, and nation is on a pathway that leads to the realization that they are part of the one humanity and one world. Some are nearer to this realization than others. But the destination is guaranteed. Practice recognizing (and intelligently nurturing) the divine or spiritual aspect within each, unifying each to all that is.

> ➢ *ASK: In this moment, how can I help others acknowledge and express their higher spiritual nature (and, in so doing, nurture my own divine expression)?*

Assess intent, resulting in *rightly directed intent*. Recognize when you or others are expressing as group conscious souls, promoting cooperation and synthesis, or self-conscious personalities, leading more often than not to competition and division.

> ➤ *ASK: What's motivating me to act right now, and to what extent do I understand the needs of others to ensure that my response furthers the common good rather than just my own or a specific group's interests?*

Practice (loving) detachment, resulting in *right action*. Realize how our collective thoughts, words, and actions reinforce separation rather than the goal of unity. Recognize that, through right understanding and rightly directed intent, we can help steer our relationships—whether between groups or nations—away from *separative diversity* to promote a realized *unity in diversity*.

> ➤ *ASK: What actions can I take to strengthen someone else's sense of unity, motivating a shift in their awareness that guides them toward more cooperative behavior that benefits the common good?*

Complete understanding and genuine, selfless service is the gift of self-mastery. Through practice, self-reflection, and commitment to serve, we can develop the best within ourselves in service to the whole. When these three practices are implemented consistently with time set aside for honest reflection regarding our success or failure, we will find that we develop our capacity to recognize the divine in others, identify when our thoughts, words, and deeds reinforce our sense of separateness, and make the needed adjustments that will encourage us and others to live more as group conscious souls rather than self-conscious personalities.

Of course, we can expect many missteps on the road to mastery. It is inevitably an attentiveness to right intent and rightly directed action that provides us with the experiences and wisdom to trust ourselves to choose rightly and help liberate others into more purposeful and joyful living.

Assessing our intent along the way conditions us to recognize where we are on the pathway to mastery and initiates our desire to self-correct.

Build bridges. Solutions based on these principles offer us and others a way forward (*and here's the key!*) that is self-initiated and mutually affirms our part in a greater whole.

As we recognize others' divine nature, reorient our focus from the material to the spiritual, and master our thoughts, words, and actions through the increasingly selfless sacrifice of our personal desires, aspirations, and will to benefit the common good, we build bridges linking each of us to every person, every nation, and the entire life of our planet. These bridges, self-initiated and mutually affirming, result in our collective highest good.

RIGHT RELATIONS PROTOCOL

Common Good Education's integration and fusion process consciously accelerates human development to further the right relations between people, nations, and the life of our entire planet. The Right Relations Protocol helps groups energize new thinking and activity based on a growing identification with the common good.

Individual
We understand and adapt our desires, feelings, and thoughts to serve the whole, becoming whole.

The One Humanity
We recognize our subjective spiritual Self, relating each to Humanity through increasingly spontaneous service for the common good.

The Planet
We choose to think and act to improve the lives of others and the world because we recognize ourselves as an integral part of a greater whole.

Copyright © 2024 School For Good - All Rights Reserved.

RIGHT RELATIONS PROTOCOL

1 RECOGNIZE THE MANY PATHS TO ONE TRUTH

Each of us is on some stage of the path leading to the realization that we are each a part of a greater whole.

In this moment, how can I help others acknowledge and express their higher, spiritual nature (and, in so doing, nurture my own divine expression)?

2 PRACTICE DETACHMENT

Spiritual detachment helps turn our attention away from the forms symbolizing our identity — things we own, our beliefs, our likes and dislikes — enabling us to see the unifying aspect linking each to all.

What actions can I take to strengthen someone else's sense of unity, motivating a shift in their awareness that guides them toward more cooperative behavior that benefits the common good?

3 ASSESS INTENT

A more self*less* rather than self*ish* intent increases our capacity to create workable solutions beneficial to all.

What's motivating me to act right now, and to what extent do I understand the needs of others to ensure that my response furthers the common good rather than just my own or a specific group's interests?

BUILD BRIDGES

Solutions based on these principles offer us and others a way forward (*and here's the key!*) that is <u>self-initiated</u> and <u>mutually affirms</u> our part in a greater whole.

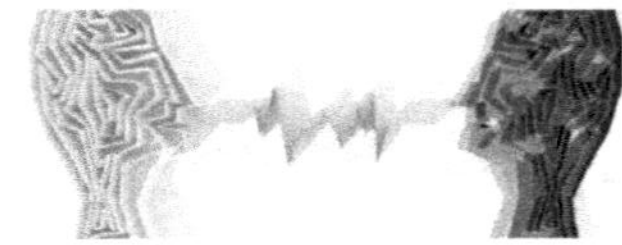

13

FINAL THOUGHTS

INTEGRATION-FUSION, THE goal of a new education, empowers children to develop a sense of direction, guiding them toward a calling and career. As they become more aware and responsive to their environment, their desire to meet the needs of their families, communities, and beyond will grow, revealing the best within them. This process of integration and fusion will not only make them definitively creative but also increase their capacity to serve.

This creativity is not just about producing art or inventions but about using their unique abilities to contribute meaningfully to society. It encompasses the *art of living* as uniquely adept individuals, aware of their capability and responsibility to the whole.

These results and greater things await us through a common good education, paving the way for a better world by nurturing a better us. We will produce human beings in the right relationship with one another, among families, one nation to another, and humanity as a whole in the right relationship with our planet.

By embedding the six pillars—real-world application, interest-based learning, autonomy and responsibility, teachers as emancipators, self-regulation and self-mastery, and prosocial relationships—into education, we cultivate a generation that values cooperation, sustainability, and equity. We ensure that the future is shaped by individuals dedicated to the well-being of all.

Education based on human development and encompassing the integration-fusion process not only prepares children for successful careers but also instills in them the values and skills needed to build a better world.

For the best prepared and academically gifted students, the new education purifies their motives and clarifies their vision, equipping them to use the resources available to serve the greater good.

For the least prepared and long neglected, the new education removes the stigmas of exclusion, allowing them to see themselves more truthfully as more than their circumstances.

For both groups of young people, the new education reorients them away from a more strictly material and, therefore, limiting self-identity towards knowledge of themselves as already *resilient*, already *worthy*, and already *whole.*

If we truly desire a new world, it must be built on a shared vision of what constitutes humanity's next step forward. These new ideals, such as compassion, collaboration, and environmental stewardship, are already emerging in the attitudes and actions of the young people we meet. Their approaches might initially seem disorienting and conflicted, as young individuals trying to find their place in a dysfunctional world often need to realize their own power and how to use it effectively to make a difference.

But the desire, hope, and *will-to-Good* are present. We must believe that.

If only we had a new education that could draw this out, we could save the children and ourselves.

The blueprint espouses a deep yearning lingering beneath the clamor in today's world of a maturing humanity, seeking a deeper connection between their inner subjective lives and their external experience. We long to bridge the gap between who we are and who we are capable of becoming to contribute to solving the problems we observe throughout every department of human life.

The new education aims to make us aware of our human and divine origins, enabling us to recognize our humanity by realizing our divinity.

Through integration fusion, we can enable students at every level of ability to harness their full potential, take the next step that is available to them, and serve as catalysts for positive change in both large and small ways, thereby creating a future where humanity thrives in harmony with itself and the planet.

Transforming education to incorporate Self-Mastery and Selfless Service for The Common Good as its foundation wherever we are and with whatever means at our disposal can become the revolutionary change needed to renew our world from the inside out.

TAISHA LALANAI RUCKER is an attorney, educator, and founder of One Humanity, a not-for-profit organization providing inspiration, education, and training to help others learn to serve the common good.

www.ingramcontent.com/pod-product-compliance
Lightning Source LLC
Chambersburg PA
CBHW050811250726
48653CB00006B/2166